MY FIRST TRIP TO
BOSNIA & HERZEGOVINA

Written by **Haris Hadžimuratović**
Illustrated by **Nina Mkhoani**

Hana

Idris

Hana is so excited: she finally gets to visit **Bosnia and Herzegovina**, the country where her family comes from! Her cousin Idris is waiting for her with her favorite Bosnian foods: **ćevapi** and **burek.**
Then it's time to explore everything!

Cathedral of the Nativity

Sahat Kula

Bey's Mosque

Vječna Vatra

Sacred Heart Cathedral

Baščaršija

Hana starts her journey in **Sarajevo,** the capital and biggest city in **Bosnia and Herzegovina.**

Sarajevo sits on the river **Miljacka** and is surrounded by mountains, but it's the old town called **Baščaršija** they explore first!

Synagogue

Vijećnica

Sebilj

You can walk down the cobblestone streets, drink tea in the cafes, and visit historical landmarks, like **Sebilj**, an ancient drinking fountain.

This is also the perfect spot to sit down and get more ćevapi (on a somun with onions, please!). Idris then introduces Hana to the best dessert ever: baklava!

Bjelašnica

Igman

Get out of the city and to the mountains that surround Sarajevo. Jump on the cable car to **Trebević** first - you can see everything from up there!

Sarajevo's mountains hosted the Winter Olympics once. Idris is already skiing down **Igman** before he runs inside to stay warm with some hot chocolate!

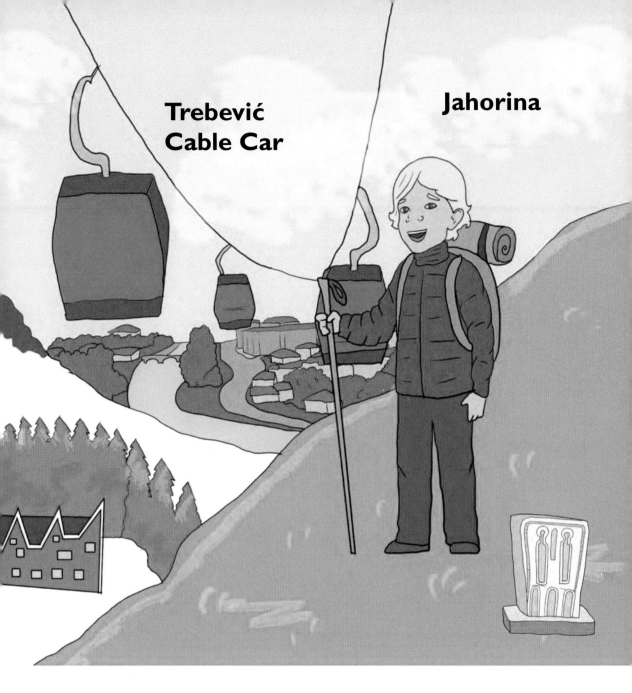

Trebević Cable Car

Jahorina

Olympic mascot **Vučko** the wolf still lives in the mountains, and Idris is looking for him. Can you find him?

In the summer, you can hike your way across the mountains - Hana got all the way to the top of **Jahorina**!

Bosnian Pyramid

Hot Springs

Now it's time to relax! Hana and Idris have found their way to one of the many **hot springs** and are swimming in the warm water.

Then it's time for another adventure: exploring the **Bosnian Pyramid**! Some say it's just a hill in the shape of a triangle, but maybe it has ancient secrets.

Sulejmanija Mosque

Ramsko Jezero

Speaking of secrets, why do you think the **Sulejmanija Mosque** is known as the colorful mosque? Go inside to find out!

Close out the day by taking a selfie at the beautiful **Ramsko Lake**.
You may not want to swim, though - the water is cold. Brrrrr!

Međugorje

Lukomir

The small town of **Međugorje** is a popular pilgrimage site.
It is visited by over a million people every year!

Lukomir is a village in two parts: its people live in one house in the summer and another in the winter. Can you find the second half on the next page?

Lukomir

Livno

Kolo

The last wild horses of Europe can be found in Bosnia in the fields near **Livno**. Idris is trying to run with them!

Dance time! The **kolo** (meaning "circle") is easy to learn and fun to do in a big group! Hana has already jumped in!

Ostrožac

Una

Štrbački Buk

Today Hana and Idris start by hiking up to the **Ostrožac** castle. They climb up the old towers and run along the ancient stone walls.

Afterward, they try to get across the river **Una** by jumping from rock to rock. Can you get all the way across? Watch out for the waterfalls!

Jajce

Pliva
Waterfall

Water Mills

While they're in the area, Hana and Idris visit the town of **Jajce**. It sits on a hill above a huge waterfall and looks especially beautiful at sunset!

Up for a picnic? Idris and Hana are! Join them on their way to the famous **Water Mills** and have lunch by the rushing water!

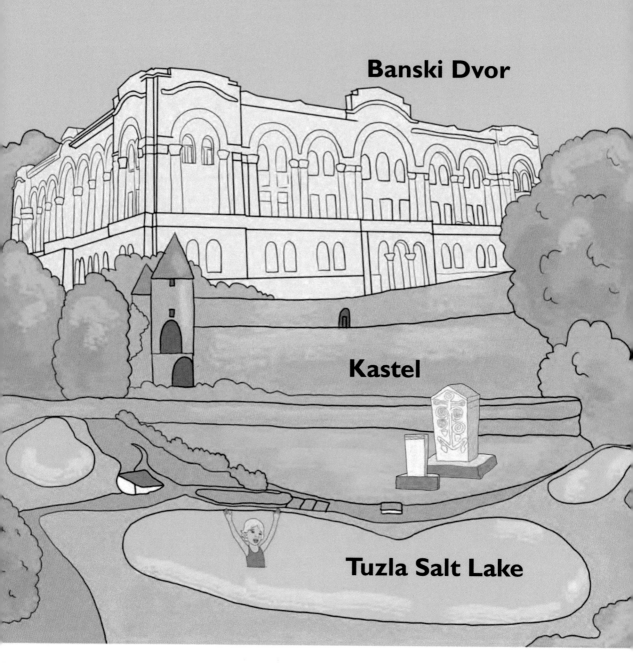

Banski Dvor

Kastel

Tuzla Salt Lake

What sounds better: an ancient fortress from Roman times or a modern palace? In Banja Luka, you can find both in the **Kastel** fortress and **Banski Dvor.**

In **Tuzla**, Hana finds a special surprise: Europe's only **salt lake** that lets you go to the beach in the middle of town!

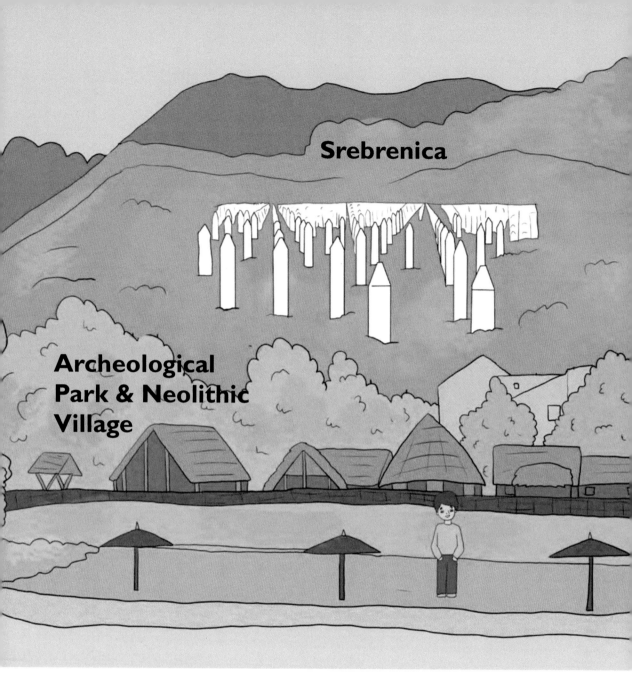

Srebrenica

Archeological
Park & Neolithic
Village

Hana dives right in because swimming is her favorite! Meanwhile Idris finds the **Neolithic Village and Archeological Park**.

Then their parents take them to visit **Srebrenica**. This is a sad but important place in Bosnia's history.

Aladža Mosque

Višegrad Bridge

In eastern Bosnia, Hana and Idris run across the famous **Višegrad Bridge.** It's a very old bridge - but not THE Old Bridge - they will visit that soon!

The **Aladža Mosque** in the town of Foča on the river Drina is another mosque that hides lots of color inside.

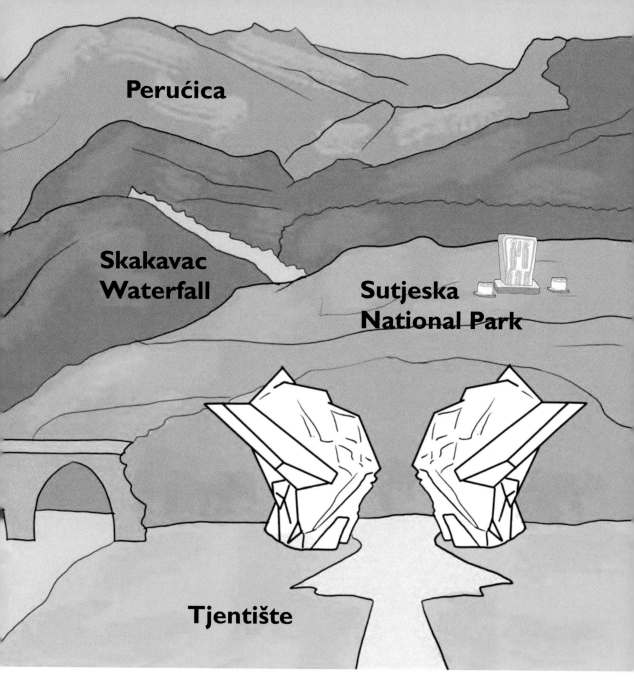

Perućica

Skakavac
Waterfall

Sutjeska
National Park

Tjentište

Next, Idris and Hana make their way through the very old **Perućica** forest. This is real wilderness - if you go, make sure you don't get lost.

The giant **Skakavac Waterfall** can help you find your way - it's as tall as 50 people!

Koski Mehmed Paša Mosque

Stari Most

In Herzegovina lies the city of Mostar, home to **Stari Most**. The name means "Old Bridge," and it really is: it's over 450 years old!

In the summer it's tradition to jump off the bridge into the river **Neretva.** Hana and Idris are just splashing in the water, but would you dare jump?

Počitelj

Blagaj Tekija

Next they hike into the hills to find **Počitelj**. This was a medieval village with a big watchtower. Can you climb all the way to the top?

Then they find a really cool building: **Blagaj Tekija**, an old monastery built right into the side of a mountain!

Neum

Vjetrenica

Up for an underground adventure? Then find your way to the **Vjetrenica Cavern**! Its name means "windy" so it's sure to be cool.

It's very deep and dark, so make sure you bring a flashlight. The cave is home to many small animals, some which only live in this cave. Try to find them!

Adriatic Sea

The best way to end any vacation is on a beach, so Hana and Idris go to **Neum** and get ready to swim in the Adriatic Sea.

Just be prepared - some are sand, but others have pebbles, so bring your flip-flops!

Psst! Did you notice some monuments hidden on the pages of this book? Those are called **stećci**. They are medieval tombstones found only in Bosnia!

There is at least one **stećak** on every spread. Did you see them all? If not, go back and try to find them!

Hana has had so much fun on her trip with Idris! She can't wait to come back and explore even more!

When are YOU going to visit **Bosnia and Herzegovina**?

Pronunciation Guide

Some names in this book are not easy to read when you don't speak Bosnian. Here's a little help.

Characters

Ć/ć: equivalent to the Italian C as in CIAO

Č/č: equivalent to TCH as in ITCH

Dž/dž: equivalent to J as in JUNGLE

Đ/đ: a softer version of J

J/j: equivalent to Y as in LAYER

LJ/lj: approximates L and Y at the same time;
    no close equivalent in English

Š/š: equivalent to SH as in ASH

Ž/ž: equivalent to the French J as in DEJA VU

Names

Aladža: ALL-ah-jah

Baklava: Bahk-LUV-uh

Banski Dvor: BAHN-ski dvor

Baščaršija: bash-CHAR-shee-yah

Bjelašnica: BYELL-ah-shnee-tsuh

Blagaj Tekija: BLAHG-eye TECK-ee-ya

Burek: BOOH-reck

Ćevapi: che-VAH-pee

Drina: DREE-na

Igman: IGG-mun

Jahorina: YAH-hoe-ree-nah

Jajce: YAH-it-say

Kastel: KAHS-tell
Kolo: KOLL-ow
Livno: LIVV-no
Lukomir: LOO-koh-mir
Međugorje: MEJ-oo-goar-yeh
Neum: NAY-um
Ostrožac: OSS-trow-zhahts
Perućica: PERR-oo-tchee-tsuh
Pliva: PLIV-ah
Počitelj: POTCH-ee-tell
Ramsko Jezero: RAHM-sko YEZZ-eh-row
Sebilj: SEBB-eel
Skakavac: SKAH-kah-vahts
Srebrenica: SREbB-ray-nee-tsuh
Stari Most: STUH-ree most
Stećak/Stećci: STETCH-ahk/STETCH-tsee
Sulejmanija: soo-lay-MAH-nee-ya
Sutjeska: SOOT-yes-kah
Štrbački Buk: SHT(E)R-bah-tchkee BOOOK
Tjentište: TYEN-teesh-teh
Trebević: tre-BEV-eech
Tuzla: TOOZ-lah
Una: OO-nah
Vijećnica: vee-YETCH-nee-tsah
Višegrad: VISH-ay-grahd
Vječna Vatra: VYETCH-nah VAH-trah
Vjetrenica: VYET-reh-nee-tsuh
Vučko: VUTCH-ko

Made in the USA
Las Vegas, NV
14 July 2022

51546782R10017